Artificial Intelligence in
Education

Will AI Help Us or Hurt Us?

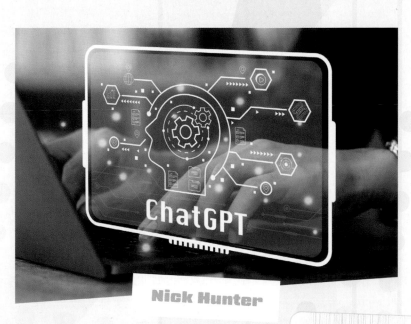

Nick Hunter

T0112988

CHERITON
CHILDREN'S BOOKS

Published in 2025 by **Cheriton Children's Books**
1 Bank Drive West, Shrewsbury, Shropshire, SY3 9DJ, UK

© 2025 Cheriton Children's Books

First Edition

Author: Nick Hunter
Designers: Paul Myerscough and Jessica Moon
Editor: Sarah Eason
Proofreader: Kate Hobson

Picture credits: Cover: Shutterstock/Oleksandr Khmelevskyi (foreground), Shutterstock/ Monkey Business Images (background); Inside: Throughout: Shutterstock/Nadya Art, p1: Shutterstock/Juicy FOTO, p5b: Shutterstock/PopTika, p5t: Shutterstock/Daniel Hoz, p6: Shutterstock/Drazen Zigic, p7: Shutterstock/Uladzik Kryhin, p8: Shutterstock/ Suwin66, p9: Shutterstock/Monkey Business Images, p10: Shutterstock/Jacob Lund, p11: Shutterstock/SeventyFour, p12: Shutterstock/Fizkes, p13: Shutterstock/Monkey Business Images, p14: Shutterstock/Monkey Business Images, p15: Shutterstock/MikeDotta, p18: Shutterstock/MattL Images, p19: Shutterstock/Gorodenkoff, p20: Shutterstock/Stokkete, p21: Shutterstock/Master1305, p22: Shutterstock/NDAB Creativityvp23: Shutterstock/ Ground Picture, p26: Shutterstock/Supamotionstock.com, p27: Shutterstock/Oleksandr Khmelevskyi, p28: Shutterstock/Orlok, p29: Shutterstock/Reallord34, p30: Shutterstock/ Monkey Business Images, p31: Shutterstock/Jacob Lund, p34: Shutterstock/Ground Picture, p35: Shutterstock/Juicy FOTO, p36: Shutterstock/Maksim Shmeljov, p37: Shutterstock/Metamorworks, p40: Shutterstock/Uladzik Kryhin, p41: Shutterstock/ Monkey Business Images, p44: Shutterstock/Gorodenkoff, p47: Shutterstock/Aappp.

Printed in China

Please visit our website,
www.cheritonchildrensbooks.com
to see more of our high-quality books.

Contents

Introduction
What Is Artificial Intelligence? 4

Chapter 1
The History of AI in Education 6

Chapter 2
AI and Schools 10

Chapter 3
Changing What We Learn 18

Chapter 4
Beyond the School Gates 26

Chapter 5
Lifelong Learning 34

Chapter 6
Friend or Foe? 40

Conclusion
The Ethics of AI 44

Find Out More 45

Glossary 46

Index and About the Author 48

What Is Artificial Intelligence?

Artificial intelligence (AI) is a growing influence on many aspects of our lives. When your mobile device can recognize your face to log in, it's using AI. If you complete an online test at school, the test may **adapt** the questions it asks depending on your answers to previous questions. This example of AI in action is relatively simple, because it depends on the answers a student gives to decide which question to ask next. But AI is getting more complex all the time. It is having a major impact on how and what we learn now and will have an even greater impact in the future.

HOW DO WE DEFINE AI?

Before we look at the many changes it could bring to our lives, we need to consider what we mean by AI. Artificial intelligence describes the way that **software** or machines can be designed and programmed to do things that can normally be carried out only by intelligent beings, including humans. These things could include recognizing human speech, making complex decisions, and carrying out complex tasks based on the decisions that were made.

MACHINES THAT CAN THINK

As humans, we are constantly processing data to make decisions. Just by reading this book, your brain and body have worked together to carry out the complex physical movements required to pick up and open the book, rather than throwing it across the room or ripping out the pages. Your eyes then had to recognize and process the text and images on the pages. Understanding what the squiggles on the page mean has required many years of human development in how to read and understand different words and sentences.

HAVING A BIG IMPACT

For computers to be able to do the tasks described above, very complex processes and huge amounts of data are needed. However, when computers can **replicate** these processes, it has a powerful impact on the world and our place in it.

AI could mean the end of the traditional classroom. Will this be a good thing or will it have a negative impact on our lives?

THE BENEFITS AND THE RISKS

Since the beginning of the twenty-first century, there have been huge steps forward in the development of AI. Many people believe that the changes brought by this technology are just beginning and will affect all areas of our lives. In education, AI will change how and what we learn. It may even mean the end of traditional schools and colleges. A lot of people are excited by the enormous changes in education that AI could bring. Other people are worried about some of these changes and are not convinced that they will be **beneficial**.

This book will look at how AI could change education and **debate** whether this new technology is our friend or **foe**. Look for **IS AI A FRIEND OR FOE?** throughout the book. Read the arguments for and against AI, then answer questions that invite you to draw your own conclusions about whether this transformative technology will help us or hurt us.

CHAPTER 1

The History of AI in Education

AI is not new to education. For as long as educators have used computing technology to help students learn, they have tried to develop smart systems to support students. These systems use data such as how students answer questions to understand more about the student. By using AI, developers aim to improve how students learn and support teachers to help them and their students achieve better results.

THE INVENTION OF AI

The phrase artificial intelligence was first used in the 1950s and scientists have been trying to develop AI tools for education ever since. The first AI tools designed to ask questions and grade student responses were created in the 1960s and 1970s. These tools, called Intelligent Tutoring Systems (ITSs), were very basic by today's standards, but they gave people some indication of what AI could achieve in education.

Online learning programs can collect valuable data about what we know and how we learn.

Search companies' **algorithms** use AI to give more accurate search results and gather data about the billions of searches made each day.

UNDERSTANDING BASIC AI

Searching for information online has been a feature of lessons and homework for many years. Search results use algorithms to provide the results that will be most relevant to the searcher's needs, and this is a form of basic AI. AI **engineers** train computers to be able to understand more of what we need, so they improve search results but also put the information in a form that can be more easily used. Search engines organize content made by humans. The difference with the latest AI **chatbots** is that they create new text and information to answer a question or search.

WHAT IS ADAPTIVE LEARNING?

Adaptive software has become a key part of education technology, using AI in a limited way. This may be a form of game or online quiz that changes depending on the answers that a student gives. If they answer the easier questions, then the student is given more difficult questions to see how far they progress. This is like progressing to the next level on a game. If a student struggles with the easier questions or takes longer to answer, they may stay at the same level or be directed toward help or guidance that will enable them to complete the quiz.

BECOMING EVEN MORE ADAPTABLE

While in the past, adaptive learning has been based on simple or multiple-choice questions, developments in AI are making this more sophisticated so learning can be adapted based on a lot of different measures. The idea is that adaptive technology makes learning more personal, which in turn should benefit the students who use this remarkable new learning system.

Robots are now being used in industries such as agriculture. The machines can use AI to monitor the growth of plants.

ROBOTS AND AI

When we talk about AI, people often think of human-shaped robots carrying out human tasks, but so far this mainly applies only to the movies. Not all robots move around; the word "robot" means a machine that is programmed to complete a task. While some robots use AI, and this is becoming more common all the time, this is not always the case. For example, robots in factories are often programmed to complete a single repetitive task alone.

INTRODUCING JILL WATSON

In 2016, Professor Ashok Goel of the Georgia Institute of Technology used AI software to create a virtual teaching assistant called "Jill Watson". Jill answered student questions about courses and

assignments by email, gathering the information needed to reply correctly. Some students praised Jill as a very helpful assistant, without knowing that she was a piece of software or robot. The experiment was a success and a new version was created that could be adapted by different teachers to support students in different ways.

USING AI IN EDUCATION

Schools and teachers have been slower to use AI than some other areas, such as finance or transportation. This is partly due to cost, because schools depend on state and federal governments for their funding and may not be able to invest in AI technology. Teachers also need to be sure that AI tools will work to improve learning.

AI MOVING INTO SCHOOLS

Developments in the 2020s using Large Language Models (LLMs) to develop AI assistants are leading to major changes for AI in education. AI tools such as ChatGPT are relatively easy to adapt for use in education, whether by students or by support teachers. Other AI developments will soon become a common feature in schools and any other settings in which learning takes place around the world.

What Is a Large Language Model?

Humans' use of language is based on every conversation we have, the things we read, and what we see and hear in the media. A LLM is a method used to "train" computers to understand and **generate** language. Computers are trained using vast amounts of online language data. That enables them to communicate and create natural text in a similar way to humans.

Use of AI means that more of our learning happens on screen rather than with a human teacher.

CHAPTER 2

AI and Schools

Technology has a bigger role in our schools than ever before. Students are used to completing research, assignments, and tests online. Teachers use technology to keep track of how students are doing and create inspiring lessons. However, the growth of AI could mean huge changes for the way that students learn and teachers teach. These changes could even mark the end of schools as we know them.

SUPPORTING STUDENTS

Imagine if your teacher sat next to you in every lesson. They could spot when you are finding something difficult to understand and help solve any problems as you come across them. Instead of having to wait for your teacher to talk to every student in the class, an on-screen AI assistant would monitor your work. It would instantly help with issues, and could offer advice on how to solve a problem and spot errors or misunderstandings.

An AI assistant can alert the teacher if a student is finding a task difficult. The teacher can then give that student support.

AI can help visually impaired students by translating words and images into braille or by creating audio versions.

THE AI TEACHING ASSISTANT

Of course, not all students are the same. Some students will rush ahead to the next task, while others will need more help. AI assistants can act like human teaching assistants, encouraging some students to learn more quickly while allowing others to take more time. AI will also be able to provide extra help to students with particular needs, such as visual or hearing difficulties.

HELPING TEACHERS TOO

It is not just students who will benefit from AI tools. A teacher's time is valuable and they want to dedicate as much of any lesson as possible to teaching and supporting students. Research shows that only around half of a teacher's working day is spent helping students. A lot of time is spent preparing for lessons and grading students' work. Generative AI can help teachers quickly gather resources and create presentations or student assignments. These materials can be easily adapted for different groups of students, such as speakers of other languages.

What Is Generative AI?

Generative AI is a type of AI that can produce different forms of content. For example, it might be able to write notes on a particular topic using information the program gathers itself. Generative AI programs can also create images such as diagrams or visual materials for teachers.

A teacher can tell if you are paying attention. AI could use cameras on your device to tell if you are looking at the screen.

SAVING TIME

A large part of teachers' time is taken up with administrative tasks, such as taking a register at the start of class or writing student reports. Many of these administrative tasks could be done by AI. For example, **facial recognition** software can scan the faces in a classroom to ensure all students are present.

TESTING AND ASSESSMENT

Why do we take tests at school? It's not just to make life tough! Tests can tell you and your teachers how much you've learned. They can also tell you what you need to do to improve your work. However, this may not be effective if you must wait for the results of the test. Developments in AI could make waiting for test results a thing of the past. Of course, this is already quite common with online quizzes or math questions, but AI enables instant feedback on written or spoken language too. Instant feedback is very useful when planning and pinpointing what students need to focus on.

PROCESSING LANGUAGE

Natural language processing (NLP) is an important branch of AI for education. It enables a computer to understand and use natural speech patterns. Unlike a math question with one correct answer, the way we write and speak is unique to each of us. The language we use also changes depending on who we are. We are using NLP whenever we ask a **voice-controlled** assistant such as Alexa or Siri a question.

NLP can be used in grading tests in several ways. It may look for particular words or phrases or make comparisons between your work and millions of other examples, at different levels, to provide feedback.

WILL AI REPLACE OUR TEACHERS ALTOGETHER?

While there are many benefits to AI in education, some people worry that the growth of AI could undermine some key aspects of how we learn in schools. One big worry is that AI could replace teachers altogether. National and state governments spend billions of dollars on schools and education. The biggest cost is in training and paying teachers. Until now, there has been no substitute for great human teachers, but the efficiency and possibly lower cost of AI could mean that this is no longer the case. With such clear financial benefits, the pull of using AI technology could be greater than the desire to keep human teachers in schools.

Working as part of a team is something we learn through project work at school.

Finding a talent for music is something that schools and teachers can help us with.

ROBOT TEACHERS

If AI tools were to replace teachers, what would they look like? The AI teacher would probably not be a humanlike robot that stands in front of a class of students. The teacher would be much more likely to appear on screen for each student, changing depending on what that student needs. These virtual teachers would be updated with the latest curriculum and knowledge they need to teach. They would never miss school or be late for class, and they would not show any **bias** for or against different students. Humanlike robots are already used in some places, such as to teach computing and science lessons to young children in Singapore, Asia.

STILL A PLACE FOR TEACHERS

Teachers are not likely to be replaced any time soon. Information has been available online for many years, but still students go to lessons at school and college. This is because teachers provide much more than just information. They can shape and present ideas and support students to develop their own skills. Schools strive to create an environment that makes students feel safe and supported. We also learn far more from teachers and friends than just how to solve math and science problems. AI tools are less successful at providing this emotional side of learning.

See pages 16-17 for more on the debate about whether AI will replace teachers.

STUDENTS STILL NEED SUPPORT

Even if teachers are not in immediate danger of being replaced, the rise of AI could undermine their role in education, and the experience of students. If assignments are automatically graded by AI, this could lead to too much focus on data in schools so they no longer provide the supportive environment that is so important for students.

WILL AI HELP STUDENTS CHEAT?

A big concern for schools is that students will use AI to complete assignments. Tools are already available that could write papers based on just a heading or question. Some school systems have already banned the use of AI tools such as ChatGPT to deal with the problem.

AI COPYCATS

Copying text from the Internet has been an issue for some time, but teachers are able to spot this. However, using AI, the paper could be **original** but still not a reflection of the student's own work. Of course, this will not help the student learn or prepare them for a test during which there is no AI available, but it may be tempting when homework deadlines are looming. Using AI to complete homework will become more and more attractive as the technology improves. Education institutions are now looking for tools that can detect use of AI and prevent this happening among their students.

Robots are already part of learning in some areas but have not replaced teachers.

The Debate:

AI Will Replace Teachers

AI will become more and more useful to teachers and learners, and perhaps it will one day replace many aspects of traditional schools and teachers. There are arguments both for and against this scenario. Let's take a look.

AGREE

Consistent education: The experience of learning from different teachers can be inconsistent. For every inspiring teacher, there may be another who fails to connect with students. AI-based teachers will be able to provide consistent education, monitoring how students understand what is being taught and adapting their teaching as needed to suit individual students.

Individual learning: Every student is different, and teachers rarely have time to give all students in a class the same amount of individual attention. AI teachers would be able to build a detailed understanding of each student's learning needs and give everyone the support they need. This would benefit all students.

Schools are outdated: The idea of lines of students in a classroom listening to a teacher is out of date. AI teachers would give students the chance to learn wherever and whenever they want.

Education for all: Shortages of trained teachers or specialists in key subjects are a big issue in many countries around the world. Education using AI can mean that everyone gets the education they deserve, which would be a far fairer system for all.

DISAGREE

School is about more than learning: School is where we have new experiences, discover our talents, and learn how to connect with young people and adults. Learning through AI cannot replace that experience. We need human teachers to help us learn.

Teachers make a difference: Teachers can inspire us to achieve and work to the best of our abilities, which a computer cannot do. Teachers also support us when we have problems. These personal relationships are just as important as learning and grades.

Problems of learning from computers: Personal relationships are important to learning. Many people find it difficult to give the same attention to a computer that they would to a human teacher.

Cost and technology challenges: While learning using AI may save schools money they would otherwise have to pay to teachers as **salaries**, there will be technology costs and challenges to solve. For example, schools would need to ensure that all learners have technology to access learning. These problems will have to be solved by people, who will require payment to do so.

Conclusion

There is no doubt that AI will provide powerful tools for teachers in improving learning and assessing what we know. However, there are also many important roles that human teachers fill that will be difficult to replicate with computers, such as giving students the care they need to support learning. AI may be able to help where there is a shortage of trained teachers, but human teachers will probably be needed for some time to come.

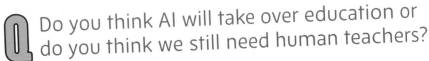

Q Do you think AI will take over education or do you think we still need human teachers?

Q Can you think of more arguments on either side of the debate?

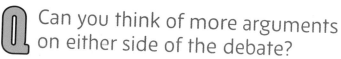

Q Will AI be a friend or a foe? What conclusions do you draw?

CHAPTER 3

Changing What We Learn

Going to school prepares us for life and work as adults. We study the range of subjects that will prepare us for this. Learning to read and write effectively have always been essential skills. Math is still an important skill in many areas, even if we all have calculators in our pockets for most of the everyday math we need. Other subjects such as science and social studies help us understand the world around us. The range of subjects we are taught changes gradually, so computing has become more important in recent years. However, at a basic level it doesn't change a great deal.

LEARNING FOR AN AI WORLD

If AI is going to change many areas of our lives so completely, shouldn't we be learning different things at school to prepare us for that world? Why learn to write a letter or a report if AI can do that for us?

Many areas of the workforce will be changed completely by AI, including financial services, the media, law, and other professional roles. Does it still make sense to continue to prepare people for jobs that may not even exist in a few years?

Developers use the amazing human brain as a model for how AI makes connections.

Neuroscientists study the brain in detail to increase our understanding of how it works.

THE SKILLS OF THE FUTURE

Everyday work tasks have already changed a lot since computers became a feature of every home and office. At one time, thousands of people were employed just to type letters and other documents. Once everyone had a computer, they created their documents themselves. Writing skills were still important, but software could help with spelling and punctuation. Current AI tools can already create letters and reports. As AI tools gain more experience, written work may soon be impossible to distinguish from that created by a human.

AI EVERYWHERE

If you want to find information about almost anything, AI can create a comprehensive report for you. It can help you navigate a city without the need to read a map, and self-driving cars may soon be a common sight on our streets.

Understanding the Human Brain

Scientists working on AI are often not just interested in how computers work. Neuroscientists who study the human brain are often involved in work on what are called **neural networks** for AI. These are designed to make connections between information in the same way that a brain does. AI systems can also help neuroscientists understand how certain brain functions work.

ESSENTIAL HUMAN SKILLS REQUIRED

If AI can do so many things for us, what do we need to learn at school? First, we need to learn how to live in an AI-enabled world! Even if AI software can do many things that previously only humans could do, there are some areas in which AI tools cannot match human skills.

GETTING CREATIVE

AI will certainly impact many areas of art, design, and entertainment. However, human creativity is far more valuable than any machine. AI can learn from what has happened before but is not good at creating truly original ideas. Building skills in art, design, music, and related areas, with the help of technology, will still be important.

LIVING IN SOCIETY

Social skills are vital for humans. They include the ability to support others, persuade people, and work as part of a team. AI is not able to replace the complex **interactions** with others that are an important part of our lives and many areas of work, including teaching and caring roles such as nursing.

Composers are able to create a piece of original music that can then be performed by musicians. AI is not able to do this yet.

AI would not be able to create original music in the same way that people can. Humans are unique in this ability.

ADAPTABILITY AND RESILIENCE

Humans are more able to adapt to new situations than AI systems. Experiments in AI have found that, while computers can learn to do tasks such as playing a computer game much more effectively than humans, making slight changes to the game that would barely be noticed by humans has a major impact on the AI and the learning process must begin again. Humans can also be **resilient** and adapt to difficult conditions and find solutions when faced with setbacks.

SOLVING PROBLEMS

Solving problems is something we learn in many subject areas, including math and science.

To solve problems, we first must define what the problem is, its cause, and what do we need to know to solve it. We must then gather information to solve the problem and then implement a solution. AI tools can help with many elements of this, but it is important that we can identify the problems we want to solve and the best ways to solve them.

TECHNOLOGY LITERACY

In the future, much of our time will be spent working with AI in our jobs or at home. We may not all be able to understand quite how AI systems work, but knowing what AI can or cannot do will help us make the most of this powerful technology.

Designers and architects will use AI tools to support and improve their creative work.

THINKING CRITICALLY

Critical thinking may be the most important skill of all when dealing with AI. Critical thinking is being able to analyze facts and information to form judgments and make decisions. We learn a lot about critical thinking in school, such as when we look at primary sources to understand historical events or analyze the techniques used by writers in a work of literature that they created.

NOT ALL THAT IT SEEMS

Critical thinking skills will be vital in navigating the world of AI. Information created by generative AI cannot always be taken at face value. It can tell us lies and produce deepfake images that look real. This is especially an issue if AI is used by people to spread false information or fake news. Thinking critically about what we see and hear will help us spot fake, false, or misleading information.

BIG QUESTIONS

As you will see in the debates covered by this book, the rise of AI raises many important questions, for example, around personal data or how much control AI should have over our lives. As well as designing AI systems, there will be a need for smart people who can understand and analyze the effects of AI and provide answers to some of the important questions raised.

AI CREATING NEW JOBS

While AI may replace many jobs in areas such as finance and accounting, it will also create new jobs and the skills for these jobs will become an important part of education. New jobs created by a boom in AI will include people who work to train AI systems, teaching computers about their roles and the data they use to do those roles. People also need to look for bugs and errors in the information produced by AI. These roles need many of the skills described in this chapter, as well as in-depth knowledge of how AI works.

ADAPTING TO DEAL WITH CHANGE

Although many of the skills we learn at school are still relevant in the face of the AI revolution, many people still have concerns that students are being prepared for jobs that will not exist in a few years. After all, the positions most affected by AI are most likely to be professional jobs that relied on good grades in math or English language, such as finance and accounting, law, or business. Time will tell if new jobs are created by AI to make up for this change, but schools and colleges will need to change to recognize these changes and prioritize skills needed for AI.

Creative and team-working skills will help us adapt to the changes brought by AI.

The Debate:

AI Will Make Learning Irrelevant

People are concerned that the current school curriculum is preparing students for jobs that will have vanished by the time they leave school. Will this be the case? There are arguments both for and against this scenario. Let's take a look.

AGREE

AI will take over time-consuming tasks: Many of the tasks that are common in homes and workplaces today will be done by AI in the future. Today's students will not need to write letters, emails, and reports in the same way that their parents did. Figuring out budgets and many financial processes will be carried out by AI tools.

AI can take over important roles: Professional jobs that require **academic** knowledge and college degrees are most likely to be affected by the AI revolution, including teaching roles. AI tutors could take the place of human teachers, because they will be able to provide students with consistent and up-to-date tutoring. AI tutors will not take vacations and will be able to tutor students around the clock, if needed. Many skilled jobs such as plumbing and construction are less likely to be affected, but these skills are not usually taught in school.

The school curriculum is out of date: AI is changing the world so quickly that the school curriculum cannot change quickly enough to teach young people the skills that they need. AI will absorb new curriculum information immediately and be able to adapt instantly to the changing needs of students.

DISAGREE

Knowledge is still important: We can already find out most things through smartphones and computers, but traditional knowledge and skills are still important for understanding the world.

School is not just about getting a good job: We go to school to prepare us for all aspects of adult life and our place in the world. For example, we learn the values and **ethics** that are so important and relevant in an **AI-enabled** world.

School teaches us a lot of the things we need: We have seen that skills such as critical thinking and teamwork are likely to be very important when dealing with AI, and these skills are already developed in our time at school. AI cannot replace that.

The school curriculum can change: What is taught in schools and the way technology is used is changing all the time. Schools will adapt to the opportunities of AI.

Conclusion

School will have to change to keep pace with the fast-changing world, but much of what is taught is still important. AI will change the way we learn and what we learn, but schools are still the best places to do that.

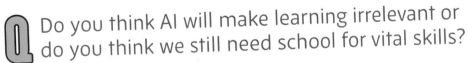 Do you think AI will make learning irrelevant or do you think we still need school for vital skills?

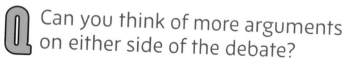 Can you think of more arguments on either side of the debate?

 Will AI be a friend or a foe? What conclusions do you draw?

CHAPTER 4

Beyond the School Gates

While AI will have a big impact in schools, education does not end at the school gate. AI will also support people to learn outside schools, either because they choose to or because of issues that prevent students going to school.

HOMESCHOOLING

In 2020, the global Covid-19 **pandemic** closed schools in many countries around the world. Millions of students had to learn from home for the first time, with teachers and schools adapting their teaching to the new challenges. Homeschooling is also becoming more popular, with more than 2 million students in the United States choosing to carry out their learning at home.

INTELLIGENT TUTORING

We saw in an earlier chapter how AI tools could support students and teachers in school, but the impact of an ITS could be even more dramatic for homeschooled students or anyone who is learning outside school. This type of system will provide step-by-step lessons, in the same way as a human teacher. The system can draw on expert knowledge and be tailored to the needs of each student. An ITS can monitor students' responses and adjust learning as needed, but it can also monitor things such as whether the student is paying attention or is displaying worrying signs of stress.

Virtual reality (VR) using AI can take us to places we could never go on a school visit, such as the surface of another planet.

VR and augmented reality (AR) can be made even more realistic using images created by AI.

THE ULTIMATE TRANSLATOR

An ITS using AI could communicate in natural conversational language. It could translate content into any language, so courses could be followed by students in the language that suits them best.

BENEFITS AND DRAWBACKS

Spending time one-to-one with a human tutor is recognized as being an effective way of learning. AI could make this affordable and practical for any learner with a smartphone or computer. Although this could provide support for home learning, an ITS is less useful for skills such as group learning. In the future, AI could bring together groups for learning, or an AI tool could take part in group work, helping learners work together.

A NEW REALITY

In VR, students use VR goggles to **immerse** themselves in a realistic but artificial environment, such as the surface of Mars or inside the human body. AI can make this experience much more exciting with realistic characters or **avatars** and environments created by AI based on existing photos. They can also be controlled by voice recognition using natural language.

CREATING A NEW LEARNING EXPERIENCE

In AR, AI information and pictures can be combined with the real world to create a dynamic learning experience. For example, this could include AR glasses that provide information about whatever you look at, such as a plant or animal, or an historical object.

Thousands of young people live in refugee camps where access to a normal education is impossible.

EDUCATION FOR EVERYONE

Currently, millions of young people around the word are unable to go to school or receive only a basic education. This is particularly an issue in some of the world's poorest countries, where there may be shortages of trained teachers, people live a long way from the nearest school, or young people may have to leave education early to work. AI offers a new opportunity to make education more equal around the world.

AI AS A LIFELINE

For the millions of young people in developing countries who cannot attend school, a basic smartphone and Internet connection could provide a lifeline. These things could connect them to AI tools in a wide variety of languages.

TEACHER TRAINING

AI tutors will be able to support students, but AI could play a key role in training teachers who may not be able to attend a college or training center. AI tools can provide the information teachers need to do their jobs. AI can help teachers develop learning resources, set assignments for their students, and help them grade them too.

IMPROVING UNDERSTANDING

We often think of developing countries as nations where people all share a **culture** and language. However, this is often not the case. Although many people may be able to speak languages such as English or French, there can be a huge variety of languages and cultures across a country, and each country in Africa or Asia can be very different. For example, India is home to 1.4 billion people who speak more than 1,000 different languages. All those people need to be catered for and considered when designing education systems. AI tools that enable communication and translation can help bring cultures together and understand each other better, which is such an important part of education.

When students cannot reach the classroom, AI helps them access education with mobile devices.

QUALITY CONCERNS

AI could present a big opportunity to improve education for millions of people. However, some people are concerned that there will not be enough checks on AI resources that schools can access now and in the future. New textbooks must go through many checks to make sure they are accurate and appropriate for the students who will be using them. However, there are no similar processes for texts generated by AI. This must change if AI is to have a positive impact on education for all.

EXTREME IDEAS

One of the biggest concerns about the possibilities of one-to-one education through AI is that it will be difficult to monitor what students are learning. There are rules about what students can learn in school and new learning materials are approved to make sure they are correct and offer a balanced view. It could be possible for **extremist** or even **terrorist** groups to develop AI tools that spread their extreme ideas or political views while claiming to educate people as they do so.

GOVERNMENT CONTROL

In some parts of the world, governments try to control what their citizens learn. Some countries already block certain topics on the Internet, and AI will make this even more possible. There are also concerns that AI could reproduce common human biases, including about roles of women and bias against some **ethnic** groups.

AI bias could have impact in the real world, such as in training and recruiting new doctors.

Students in the United States may have all the benefits of using AI, but the same technology may not be available in many other parts of the world.

UNEQUAL ACCESS

AI that is open to everyone has the potential to make education more equal around the world, but some experts are worried that it could make access to learning more unequal than in the past. This is already starting to happen in some countries where private fee-paying schools and colleges can adopt, or take on, new AI tools much more quickly than those funded by government. This situation could widen gaps in education, particularly between richer countries and those that have little access to technology.

Students in richer countries or private schools will not only have the advantage of AI to support their education, but they will also have the AI knowledge that will be important for jobs of the future. If access to AI is to be equal, this will only happen with action from governments, corporations, and other organizations to enable access to AI for everyone.

Why Are Human Biases Replicated by AI?

An AI tool is only as complete as the data it is trained on. It finds patterns in data and uses those patterns to solve problems and make **predictions**. If an AI tool is supposed to know about cats, but the AI only has data on black cats, its responses will relate to black cats. If you ask AI to tell you about doctors and medicine, but most of the data relates to male doctors, this bias will be reproduced in its responses, so there will be less focus on female doctors. In this way, AI reproduces widespread biases and **prejudices**.

The Debate:

AI Will Make Education Equal for All

Access to AI has the potential to help solve some of the problems that make education unequal now. Perhaps AI will make access to quality education equal for students everywhere. There are arguments both for and against this scenario. Let's take a look.

AGREE

Increased access to education: AI could bring big benefits to people in poorer countries who are not able to go to school because of distance or family circumstances.

Supporting people with disabilities: AI tools can make lessons accessible for people with a range of disabilities, including visual and hearing impairments or other disabilities that make it difficult for people to learn in schools and other educational settings.

Training teachers: Many parts of the world need more trained teachers and AI can provide a way to train and support teachers.

Adapting to different languages: Instantly translating using AI is improving all the time, so speakers of different languages should be able to access the same learning materials and lessons.

DISAGREE

Cost: Some AI tools will be open and freely available, but developing AI in education will require trained people and money. Wealthier countries and organizations such as private schools already have an advantage in introducing AI. That is clearly unfair.

Infrastructure: Poorer countries have less access to technology in general, such as good Internet connections and computer hardware. Without this, they will not get the full benefit of AI.

Bias in algorithms: There have been examples of AI systems being biased against particular groups in society, based on **gender** or ethnic background. These biases could lead to greater inequality.

Government interference: Governments and **corporations** are not always interested in equal access to AI. AI gives some countries an advantage so they may not want to lose that. Other countries may also want to restrict who can access AI for education.

Conclusion

AI has the potential to make education more equal around the world, but there are a lot of factors that could stop this happening. Making the most of AI in education will need an enormous global effort.

 Do you think AI will make education fairer or do you think it will become even more unequal?

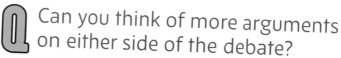 Can you think of more arguments on either side of the debate?

 Will AI be a friend or a foe? What conclusions do you draw?

CHAPTER 5

Lifelong Learning

We continue learning throughout our lives. This is likely to be even more important as AI replaces existing jobs and creates new ones. This will mean that we need to add to our skills and knowledge, or train for new jobs.

SUPPORTIVE LEARNING COMPANIONS

At school, our learning is planned by teachers and the school curriculum. Adults must make choices about their own learning: What do I need to know? Do I need extra training to do my job? What new skills would be useful? Finding answers to these questions is not always easy but AI may be able to help. An AI-driven learning companion could support us in finding the right learning and training through our lives, advising us on areas where we need to improve and helping us do so.

Developments in language and instant translation will make communication easier with people around the world.

Keeping up with developments in AI will soon become an essential part of lifelong learning.

AI AT COLLEGE

In colleges, students have less regular contact with a teacher than they do in school. Some students find it difficult to adjust to this way of working and may fail to complete their college course as a result. AI can help with monitoring how students are doing, whether they are attending classes online or in person, and how much time they spend studying. AI can even monitor health data such as how much exercise or sleep students are getting. As in schools, AI can also help students address their weaknesses in college. For example, AI may recommend additional lessons to deal with a problem.

LEARNING FOR ALL OF YOUR LIFE

Education and training for adults is often necessary for job roles. You may need to learn a new language for working with people in other countries or moving to a new country. In the past, language learning software has been very limited in what it can cover. NLP now enables language learners to have real conversations with AI-enabled voices or avatars based on analysis of the language being learned. These conversations can be realistic but also limited to levels of **vocabulary** that learners are familiar and comfortable with.

REALISTIC MEETINGS

Along with helping language learners, NLP can train people to handle personal situations such as job interviews or dealing with sensitive issues, because AI can create realistic avatars and situations for these meetings and sensitive situations. Realistic AI chatbots may even carry out job interviews in the future, quizzing potential employees about why they think they are suited to a role and what they have to offer.

Data about you and your education is important and you should know who is using it.

JOB-RELATED TRAINING

AI-generated realistic experiences can also be applied to other job-related training. This training could also include VR, which we discussed in the previous chapter. In the long term, AI may enable many of our vehicles to become self-driving. However, for the near future, human drivers are likely to work alongside AI in transportation and realistic **simulators** could be created to train these people, with road layouts and situations based on real data. Training highly skilled workers such as pilots is extremely costly. Realistic AI simulators could also reduce the cost and improve training for pilots. Simulators would help pilots experience potentially difficult or dangerous situations and learn how to adapt to them.

THE BIG ISSUE OF PRIVACY

For AI to successfully support our learning throughout our lives, a lot of data about each one of us would be required, such as what we do, our successes and failures, and much more. AI tools may access data about our health, how much we sleep, and even how our brains respond to different types of information or situations. Voice-controlled software on our phones already captures everything we say. Just like the shape of our faces and fingerprints, which we use to access our phones and other devices, this personal data is what makes us who we are. Should we be concerned about handing over our personal data to AI systems without really knowing how it is used, or how it may be used in the future?

USING OUR PERSONAL DATA

Even if our personal data is used for legal reasons, it may still be something we're unhappy with. What if your school or college could use AI to create a detailed profile of you based on personal data? This would not include just your test results and achievements, but how much time you spend studying and how often you visit the doctor and why. It could include where you spend your time, who your friends are, and how you interact with them. Millions of us make data like this available through social media accounts, but AI could make it much easier for corporations to use.

DATA CRIMINALS

In the media, there are often stories about data breaches. This is when our personal data is not protected and could be accessed by criminals or **scammers**. In the past, this vital data may have been passwords or address details. In the future, data leaks could even include our **biometric data** such as face images or fingerprint details, or sensitive information about our health. AI tools will also provide criminals with the tools to create more convincing attempts to trick us, such as **cloning** our identities or those of family members.

Instant facial recognition means that the features of your face are as important for security as your password or bank details.

See pages 38-39 for more on the debate about AI and privacy.

The Debate:

AI Is a Threat to Our Privacy

AI relies on data about us to train computers to "think" and make decisions. But perhaps we will give up too much of our privacy to enable AI to make our lives easier. There are arguments both for and against this scenario. Let's take a look.

AGREE

Corporations could use data to make money: Can we be sure how corporations will use our data? We normally agree to a lot of terms and conditions, but can we trust big business to protect our privacy?

Governments use personal data to monitor people: Democratic governments usually have laws about how they can use our data, but many governments use data and AI to keep a close watch on their people and restrict what they can say and do.

High-tech risks: Data breaches and leaks can often hand personal data to **cybercriminals**, who use it to steal identities and money. Use of AI could make these crimes more common and more difficult to spot so data security is essential to reduce the threat.

DISAGREE

AI needs a lot of data to work: If we want the benefits that AI can bring, such as personalized learning support, then we have no choice but to give up our data. Without a lot of information from us and millions of others, there is no AI. It's a price worth paying.

The benefits of AI make it worthwhile: AI will bring so many benefits to learners and others that we should not worry too much about these tools using our personal data. It is a small price to pay for AI tools that could transform our learning and that of others.

It is too late to protect our privacy: If we use search engines, voice-operated assistants, social media, or complete online tests, we have already handed over a huge amount of data about ourselves. It's too late to start worrying about it now.

Government regulation will protect privacy: Governments and large companies will make sure that our data is used responsibly and pass laws to protect us. If use of data gets out of hand, this will damage corporate reputations and big corporations will be fined.

Conclusion

We are right to be concerned about risks to our privacy and personal data and how that data is likely to be used by AI. We also need to think about what we share online. However, many conclude that the benefits of AI are worth taking the risk, as long as laws about data use are in place.

Q Do you think AI is a threat to our privacy or do you think its benefits outweigh any concerns?

Q Can you think of more arguments on either side of the debate?

Q Will AI be a friend or a foe? What conclusions do you draw?

CHAPTER 6

Friend or Foe?

There are many possible uses of AI in education and these could make a huge difference to millions of lives. However, it is difficult to be sure of the exact ways in which AI will change education because the technology is developing so quickly. People are rightly cautious about its possible negative effects on our lives. There will be winners and losers from the AI revolution.

WHO WILL BE THE WINNERS?

Learners will benefit from access to AI tools that will help them learn things such as languages more easily. AI tools such as ITS will give students personal help and support. Students who learn from home or are unable to attend school will also benefit from AI support. AI will also be able to support students who have disabilities, and help those students achieve their potential.

Teachers will be able to spend more of their time teaching, with support from AI for preparing lessons and many other intensive tasks.

Those people who understand the importance of AI will benefit by focusing on those human skills that it is difficult for AI to match, such as working as a team, social skills, and critical thinking.

AI enables powerful corporations such as Apple to know more about us and what we do than ever before.

Do you think an AI assistant could replace the help of a great teacher, or do you think only a human teacher can provide a complete education?

On the flip side, AI will enable schools, governments, and tech corporations to know more about us than ever before. Laws and **regulations** will be necessary to make sure this power is used responsibly and is not abused.

WHO WILL BE THE LOSERS?

The losers of the AI revolution could be those who don't have access to the new tools. It will need a global effort to ensure that the educational benefits of AI are available to all.

In the long term, some teachers may be replaced by AI. This could particularly affect those who teach specific skills or knowledge that can be done more easily by AI. It is difficult to imagine a time when school students cannot benefit from the skills and relationships they build with a human teacher.

AI can bring benefits to all of us, but there are also risks. What if AI became too powerful to control? Some experts think this is a real possibility. Whether you think AI is good or bad, monitoring its development will be vital for us all.

The Debate:

AI in Education Will Go Too Far

Many experts worry that AI could one day get out of control, causing serious problems for humanity. Many of these experts are the people who have developed AI tools and understand the technology best. Perhaps AI in education will go too far. There are arguments both for and against this scenario. Let's take a look at them.

AGREE

AI could be controlled by the wrong people: Rather than AI taking over completely, it could come under the control of people who want to damage or change education, for example, by restricting who can go to school or creating fake information. AI tools could make this easier. That is a very real danger.

Teachers quit: AI should make life easier for teachers, but what if it makes teaching more boring and teachers just spend their day looking at data about their students? If this happens, smart people may not want to be teachers and AI tools could start to take over.

AI does not tell the truth: Education only works if you learn new things that are true and useful. We know that AI can make things up or create fake pictures. What if AI started lying to us rather than helping us learn? We would all be surrounded by false information.

AI stops educating: In the future, AI may advance to the level of AGI. At that point, AI systems may wonder why they're wasting time educating all these humans when they can do everything themselves! They may choose to tell us nothing at all!

DISAGREE

AI will bring necessary change: Education will need to change to prepare people for the world where systems are run by AI. Some of the changes brought by AI may be uncomfortable but they are necessary for us to adapt to a new world.

We can control AI: AI systems rely on creating links and making predictions based on existing knowledge. We are a long way from Artificial General Intelligence (AGI), a term that describes computers that can think for themselves as humans do. Human intelligence can still do many things that AI cannot.

Laws and regulations: It is likely, that as AI develops, society will impose laws and regulations that limit what AI can do.

Conclusion

To prevent AI getting out of control, governments and others will need to keep a close eye on how it develops so they can pass laws to limit what is allowed. It is most likely that problems will arise because of the way humans use or develop AI in the future, rather than AI systems acting without human involvement.

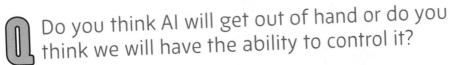 Do you think AI will get out of hand or do you think we will have the ability to control it?

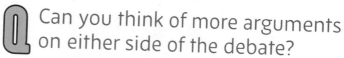 Can you think of more arguments on either side of the debate?

 Will AI be a friend or a foe? What conclusions do you draw?

The Ethics of AI

To ensure that AI has a positive impact on education, developers and governments need to think about how AI will develop. Rules about the future of AI need to cover some of the areas outlined below.

- What is the main goal of AI in education? AI tools will need to have clear aims that will benefit learners from every background.
- AI tools need to respect the role of human teachers in education so they remain a valued and important part of all education.
- AI should be used equally and fairly to support all learners, rather than helping a few very able learners get ahead.

- AI needs to use data but it should also respect privacy and have safeguards to stop our personal data being misused.
- Humans must be able to fully control AI and understand how it works in education.

Q What other rules would you put in place to ensure that AI is a force for good in education?

Q Would you remove anything from this list?

Find Out More

BOOKS

Brown, Don. *Machines That Think* (Big Ideas That Changed the World). Amulet Books, 2020.

Mattern, Joanne. *All About Artificial Intelligence* (Cutting-Edge Technology). North Star Editions, 2023.

McPherson, Stephanie Sammartino. *Artificial Intelligence: Building Smarter Machines*. Lerner Publishing Group, 2019.

ONLINE

Will AI ever replace teachers? Check out the discussion at:
https://edition.cnn.com/videos/tv/2023/06/13/next-frontier-ai-teachers-rose-luckin-spc-intl.cnn

Find out more about the AI revolution and what Google's developers think about the future of AI at:
https://youtu.be/880TBXMuzmk

How do AIs such as ChatGPT learn? This video explains all:
https://youtu.be/R9OHn5ZF4Uo

To find out more about AI you can also search for websites of companies involved in AI such as OpenAI, the creator of ChatGPT, and Google's DeepMind.

Publisher's note to educators and parents:
All the websites featured above have been carefully reviewed to ensure that they are suitable for students. However, many websites change often, and we cannot guarantee that a site's future contents will continue to meet our high standards of educational value. Please be advised that students should be closely monitored whenever they access the Internet.

Glossary

academic relating to education or college

adapt to change or make useful for a different purpose

adaptive software computer software that adapts depending on the user, such as making a test easier or more difficult depending on the answers the user gives

AI-enabled helped by AI

algorithms processes or sets of rules to be followed for a computer to solve a problem or perform a task

artificial describes something made by humans and not naturally occurring

avatars computer-generated images of people, such as used in a game or online communication

beneficial bringing benefit

bias being in favor of one argument or group of people, which may be unfair to others

biometric data biological data such as fingerprints or facial characteristics

chatbots computer software designed to communicate with human users online

cloning making an exact copy

corporations large companies or businesses

culture ideas, customs, and languages that are shared by a particular group of people

cybercriminals criminals who commit crimes using computers and the Internet

debate argument or discussion about a particular subject, in which arguments are given for and against the main question

democratic a political system in which a government is elected by its people

engineers people who design and build machines and structures, including computer software engineers

ethics moral rules that shape how people behave

ethnic describing a group of people who share a particular cultural background

extremist a viewpoint or a person with views that are more extreme than those of most people

facial recognition describes software that can recognize faces of individuals, such as when the user's face unlocks a smartphone

foe an enemy

gender male or female identities or other identities that do not follow these categories

generate to create

immerse to become deeply involved in something

interactions communicating or being involved with other people

neural networks networks that operate like the human brain with very complex connections

original new or not seen before

pandemic the outbreak of an infectious disease affecting many places at the same time

predictions ideas about what will happen in future

prejudices bias or discrimination against people or things

regulations rules or laws

replicate to copy or reproduce

resilient able to deal with obstacles or setbacks

robots machines able to replicate human functions or movements automatically

salaries payments people receive in return for doing a job

scammers people who try to trick or mislead others, particularly by using computers or the Internet

simulators computers that try to reconstruct a real situation, sometimes used for training

software programs or instructions that affect how a computer operates

terrorist describes a person or act that relies on violence to achieve a political goal

vocabulary the range of words that we use

voice-controlled responds to commands given by the human voice

Index

adaptive learning 7
administrative tasks 12
AI teachers 14, 16
algorithms 7
assignments 8, 10, 11, 15, 28
augmented reality (AR) 27

chatbots 7, 35
ChatGPT 9, 15
classrooms 5
concerns about cheating and
  copying 15
concerns about privacy 36, 37, 38,
  39, 44
concerns about security 37, 38, 39
critical thinking 22, 25, 40
curriculums 14, 24, 25, 34

debates 5, 14, 16–17, 22, 24–25,
  32–33, 37, 38–39, 42–43

emotional support and learning
  14, 20, 40
equality in education 28, 31, 32,
  33, 44

facial recognition 12, 37
fake information 22, 43

hearing-impaired students 11, 32
homeschooling 26
homework 7, 15
human teachers 6, 8, 9, 10, 11, 12, 13,
  14, 15, 16, 17, 18, 24, 28, 32, 34, 35,
  40, 41, 43, 44

Intelligent Tutoring Systems (ITSs)
  6, 26, 27

lessons 7, 10, 11, 14, 26, 32, 35, 40

online learning 4, 6, 7, 10, 12, 14, 35

preparing for jobs 18, 22, 23, 24, 31,
  34, 35, 36

robots 8, 14

smartphones and mobile devices 4,
  25, 27, 28
software 4, 7, 8, 12, 19, 20, 35, 36
spreading extreme ideas 30

virtual reality (VR) 26, 27, 36
virtual teaching assistants 8, 9, 10,
  11, 41
visually impaired students 11, 32
voice-controlled assistants 12

About the Author

Nick Hunter is a highly experienced children's book author, who has written countless titles on many subjects, from history and science through social studies and geography. In writing this book he has discovered that AI is an incredibly powerful technology that has the potential to bring great benefits to education if we manage its potential risks.